By the Editors of Best Recipes

Best Recipes

APPETIZERS

COOKBOOK

SMITHMARK

INTRODUCTION

Great appetizers make the party and what better place to find dozens of fabulous recipes than this unique collection of award-winning appetizers. Gathered from a variety of recipe contests and cook-offs across America, it represents some of the most exciting and delectable party treats around! These original prize-winning recipes were created by home cooks like you. The names of these champion cooks, as well as the contests they entered, are included for each of the fabulous recipes.

This edition published in 1991 by SMITHMARK Publishers Inc., 112 Madison Avenue, New York, NY 10016

SMITHMARK books are available for bulk purchase for sales promotion and premium use. For details write or telephone the Manager of Special Sales, SMITHMARK Publishers Inc., 112 Madison Avenue, New York, NY 10016. (212) 532-6600.

Photography on pages 9, 17, 19, 23, 37 and 39 by Vuksanovich/Chicago.

Remaining photography by Sacco Productions Limited/Chicago.
Photographers: Ray Cheydler
              Laurie Proffitt
Photo Stylist/Production: Paula Walters
              Betty Karslake

Food Stylists: Janice Bell
            Donna Coates

ISBN: 0-8317-0597-3

Library of Congress Catalog Card Number: 90-64444

Pictured on the front cover (*clockwise from top right*): Shrimp Mold (*page 76*), Hot 'n' Honeyed Chicken Wings (*page 74*), Scallops á la Schaller (*page 84*), Clams Casino (*page 88*) and Patrician Escargots (*page 48*).

Pictured on back cover (*from top to bottom*): Southwestern Snack Squares (*page 72*), Fall Harvest Popcorn (*page 56*), Picante Onion Soup (*page 4*) and Southwest Appetizer Cheesecake (*page 36*).

First published in the United States.

Manufactured in Yugoslavia.

8   7   6   5   4   3   2   1

By the Editors of Best Recipes

Best Recipes

APPETIZERS

COOKBOOK

SENSATIONAL SOUPS

Does chopping or slicing onions make you cry? It is probably due to an enzyme called alliinase. When exposed to the air through peeling or chopping it can irritate the tear ducts causing your eyes to water. Sometimes chilling the onion before cutting can reduce the effects of alliinase.

Picante Onion Soup

◆ Joyce Lee Sproul from Pembroke Pines, Florida was the grand prize winner in the Pace® Picante Sauce "Pick Up the Pace" Recipe Contest sponsored by Pace Foods, Inc.

Makes 6 servings

   3 cups thinly sliced onions
   1 clove garlic, minced
   ¼ cup butter or margarine
   2 cups tomato juice
   1 can (10½ ounces) condensed beef broth
   1 soup can water
   ½ cup Pace® picante sauce
   1 cup unseasoned croutons (optional)
   1 cup (4 ounces) shredded Monterey Jack
      cheese (optional)
      Additional Pace® picante sauce

Place onions, garlic and butter in 3-quart saucepan. Cook over medium-low heat about 20 minutes, stirring frequently, until onions are tender and golden brown. Stir in tomato juice, broth, water and ½ cup picante sauce; bring to a boil. Reduce heat and simmer, uncovered, 20 minutes. Ladle soup into bowls and sprinkle with croutons and cheese. Serve with additional picante sauce.

Note: 2⅔ cups ready-to-serve beef broth may be substituted for the condensed beef broth and water.

Chilly Cucumber Soup

♦ Joel Stephens from Nashville, Tennessee was the first prize winner in "The Secret's in the Soup" Recipe Contest sponsored by Thomas J. Lipton, Inc.

Makes about 6 servings

   2 tablespoons butter or margarine
   2 tablespoons all-purpose flour
   4 large cucumbers, peeled, seeded and finely chopped (about 3½ cups)
   ¼ cup finely chopped parsley
   ¼ cup finely chopped celery leaves
   1 envelope Lipton® Golden Onion Recipe Soup Mix
   2 cups water
   2 cups light cream or half-and-half Cucumber slices, celery leaves and lemon peel, for garnish

Melt butter in large saucepan. Stir in flour and cook over medium heat 3 minutes, stirring constantly. Add cucumbers, parsley and celery leaves. Cook over low heat 8 minutes or until cucumbers are tender. Combine soup mix and water; add to cucumber mixture. Bring to a boil, then reduce heat; cover and simmer 15 minutes. Remove from heat and set aside to cool. When cool, puree soup mixture in food processor or blender. Stir in cream; cover and refrigerate. Serve soup cold. Garnish with cucumber, celery leaves and lemon peel.

"Dearhearts" Seafood Bisque

♦ Michele Myers from San Jose, California was the first place winner at the Castroville Artichoke Festival Recipe Contest, Castroville, California.

Makes 6 servings

   2 tablespoons olive oil
   1 onion, finely chopped
   3 pounds fresh baby artichoke hearts, outer leaves removed, leaf tips trimmed and hearts cut into quarters
   2 cups chicken broth
   ½ cup white wine
   1 pound mixed shellfish (shrimp, crab, scallops), cleaned and shells removed
   1 cup heavy cream
   2 tablespoons chopped parsley
   1 teaspoon salt
   ½ teaspoon ground nutmeg
   ¼ teaspoon white pepper

Heat oil in large saucepan; add onion and cook gently for 5 minutes or until softened. Add artichokes, broth and wine. Cover and simmer 20 to 30 minutes or until artichokes are tender and a leaf pulls away easily. Process mixture in food processor or blender until smooth. Return soup to saucepan. Stir in shellfish, cream, parsley, salt, nutmeg and pepper. Simmer very gently, uncovered, over low heat 5 to 10 minutes. Do not boil or shellfish will become tough.

Peeling Tomatoes

To peel tomatoes, place them, one at a time, in a saucepan of simmering water for about 10 seconds. (Add about 30 seconds if they are not fully ripened.) Then immediately plunge them into a bowl of cold water for another 10 seconds. The skins will peel off easily with a knife. Do not add more than one tomato to the water at a time or the temperature will drop rapidly and the tomatoes will stew before their skins can be removed.

Golden Tomato Soup

◆ Kim Plotzky from Stamford, Connecticut was the sixth place winner in the *Weight Watcher's Magazine* recipe contest sponsored by the Florida Tomato Committee.

Makes 8 servings

    4 teaspoons reduced-calorie margarine
    1 cup chopped onion
    2 cloves garlic, coarsely chopped
    ½ cup chopped carrots
    ¼ cup chopped celery
    8 medium-size tomatoes, blanched, peeled,
        seeded and chopped
    6 cups chicken broth
    1 ounce uncooked rice
    2 tablespoons tomato paste
    1 tablespoon Worcestershire sauce
    ¼ to ½ teaspoon black pepper
    ½ teaspoon dried thyme
    5 drops hot pepper sauce

Melt margarine in large Dutch oven over medium-high heat. Add onion and garlic; cook and stir 1 to 2 minutes or until tender. Add carrots and celery; cook 7 to 9 minutes or until tender, stirring frequently. Stir in tomatoes, broth, rice, tomato paste, Worcestershire sauce, pepper, thyme and hot pepper sauce. Reduce heat to low; cook about 30 minutes, stirring frequently.

Remove from heat and let cool about 10 minutes. In food processor or blender, process soup in small batches until smooth. Return soup to Dutch oven; simmer 3 to 5 minutes or until heated through. Garnish as desired.

Potato Soup Plus

◆ Scottie Kuhlmann from Slidell, Louisiana
was a finalist in *The Times-Picayune Cookbook*
Recipe Contest.

Makes 12 servings

> 2 cups water
> 2 cups red potatoes, peeled and cut
>   into cubes
> 3 tablespoons butter or margarine
> 1 small onion, finely chopped
> 3 tablespoons all-purpose flour
>   Creole seasoning
>   Red and black pepper to taste
> 3 cups milk
> ½ teaspoon sugar
> 1 cup (4 ounces) shredded Cheddar cheese
> 1 cup cubed cooked ham
>   Chopped parsley, for garnish

Bring water to a boil in large saucepan. Add
potatoes and cook until tender. Meanwhile,
melt butter in large skillet over medium heat.
Add onion; cook and stir until tender but
not brown. Add flour; season with Creole
seasoning and red and black pepper. Cook
3 to 4 minutes; set aside. Drain potatoes,
reserving 1 cup liquid (add water to make 1 cup
if necessary). Gradually add potatoes, reserved
liquid, milk and sugar to onion mixture; stir
well. Add cheese and ham. Simmer over low
heat 30 minutes, stirring frequently. Garnish
with parsley.

Sherried Oyster and Brie Soup

◆ Judith Mettlin from Snyder, New York was a prize winner at the St. Mary's County National Oyster Cook-Off in Leonardtown, Maryland.

Makes 4 servings

1 quart select Maryland oysters with liquor
2 tablespoons butter or margarine
1 pound fresh mushrooms, thinly sliced
½ cup minced shallots
2 tablespoons fresh lemon juice
2 tablespoons all-purpose flour
3 cups beef broth
1 cup cream sherry, reduced to ½ cup*
4 ounces Brie cheese, rind trimmed
1 cup milk
1 cup heavy cream
Salt and pepper to taste
Chives, for garnish

Drain oysters and reserve liquor; set aside. Melt butter in large saucepan over medium-high heat. When foam subsides, stir in mushrooms, shallots and lemon juice; cook and stir 2 minutes. Sprinkle with flour; cook and stir 1 minute more. Add broth and reduced sherry. Bring to a boil; reduce heat and simmer 20 minutes.

Add Brie and stir to melt. Stir in reserved oyster liquor, milk and cream; season with salt and pepper. Heat until very hot. Do not boil. Remove from heat and add oysters. Cover and let stand until oysters are just plumped. Garnish with chives.

To reduce, simmer over medium heat until slightly thickened and reduced to desired amount.

To Make Toasted Pumpkin Seeds

Carefully separate the pumpkin seeds from fibers. Wash, drain and dry on paper towels. Coat the seeds with a small amount of vegetable oil. Add 2 tablespoons Worcestershire sauce and ½ teaspoon ground red pepper and toss to mix thoroughly. Spread seasoned seeds in a single layer on a baking sheet. Bake in 275°F oven, stirring occasionally, until golden brown.

Pumpkin Almond Bisque in Its Own Shell

♦ Caroline Hunt was a prize winner at the March of Dimes Gourmet Gala in Houston, Texas.

Makes about 8 servings

1 medium-size pumpkin
3 cups chicken broth, divided
2 tablespoons butter or margarine
3 tablespoons chopped celery
3 tablespoons chopped onion
2 tablespoons almond paste
1 tablespoon tomato paste
1½ cups light cream
3 tablespoons almond-flavored liqueur
1 teaspoon ground nutmeg
1 teaspoon pepper
 Salt to taste
 Toasted pumpkin seeds, for garnish

Cut slice from top of pumpkin. Scoop out flesh leaving shell that can be used for serving. Simmer pumpkin flesh in small amount of broth until tender. Place cooked pumpkin in food processor or blender container; process until smooth. (There should be 2 cups of pumpkin puree.) Leave puree in food processor.

Melt butter in heavy soup pot. Add celery and onion; cook over low heat 5 minutes. Add celery mixture, almond paste and tomato paste to pumpkin puree and process until smooth. Return to pot; add remaining broth and simmer over low heat 30 minutes. Stir in cream and cook until heated through. Stir in liqueur, nutmeg, pepper and salt. Pour into reserved pumpkin shell. Garnish with toasted pumpkin seeds.

Florida Cream of Avocado Soup

♦ Pat Wallace was the American Regional Cuisine Award winner at the March of Dimes Gourmet Gala in Miami, Florida.

Makes 12 servings

    6 medium-size Florida avocados
    1 cup dry white wine
    4 medium-size eggs*
    4 cups milk, divided
    1 cup chicken broth
    ½ teaspoon salt
    ¼ teaspoon white pepper
    ¼ teaspoon ground red pepper
    3 cups sour cream, divided
      Black caviar and ground red pepper,
        for garnish

Cut avocados in half lengthwise so that each half will rest evenly on a plate. Remove and discard pits. Scoop out flesh leaving ¼-inch shell; cover and refrigerate shells. Place avocado flesh and wine in food processor or blender container; process until smooth. Transfer to large bowl; set aside.

In top of double boiler, beat eggs with 2 cups of the milk. Heat slowly over hot water, stirring until mixture is thick enough to coat spoon. Remove from heat; stir in broth and set aside to cool. Stir cooled custard and seasonings into avocado mixture. Mix in 2 cups of the sour cream, stirring until smooth. Add remaining 2 cups milk. Process in small batches in food processor or blender until completely smooth. Adjust seasonings. Cover and refrigerate until very cold.

To serve, pour cold soup into avocado shells. Garnish each portion with about 1 tablespoon of the remaining 1 cup sour cream. Garnish with caviar and red pepper.

*Use clean, uncracked eggs.

Black-Eyed Pea Soup

♦ Joe Bayer from Dallas, Texas was the fourth place winner at the Black-Eyed Pea Jamboree, Athens, Texas.

Makes 12 to 16 servings

2 pounds fresh East Texas Black-Eyed Peas*
½ pound bacon, diced
4 medium-size onions, thinly sliced
4 carrots, thinly sliced
8 quarts water
2 cups thinly sliced celery
2 large potatoes, peeled and grated
2 whole jalapeño peppers
4 bay leaves
½ teaspoon dried thyme
1 meaty ham bone
Salt and pepper to taste

Clean and drain black-eyed peas; set aside. Combine bacon, onions and carrots in large saucepan. Cook and stir over medium-high heat until onions are golden. Add black-eyed peas, water, celery, potatoes, jalapeño peppers, bay leaves, thyme and ham bone. Season with salt and pepper. Cover; simmer over low heat 3 to 4 hours. Remove and discard whole jalapeños and bay leaves. Cut meat from ham bone and return meat to saucepan. Adjust seasonings; reheat if necessary.

*Fresh black-eyed peas are often available in supermarkets in the produce section. If desired, substitute 1 pound dried black-eyed peas, cooked, for the fresh.

ELEGANT STARTERS

Clarifying Butter

Clarified butter is what remains after removing protein and milk solids from butter. It is simple to make and has the advantage of cooking at high temperatures without burning. Melt the butter over low heat. Skim off the white foam that forms on top, then strain the clear, golden clarified butter through cheesecloth into a container. Discard the milky residue at the bottom of the pan. You can make a large quantity of clarified butter at one time. It will keep, covered, in the refrigerator for up to 2 months.

Scampi alla "Fireman Chef"

♦ Jim Neil from Gilroy, California was a finalist in the Gilroy Garlic Festival Recipe Contest, Gilroy, California. Courtesy of the Gilroy Garlic Festival Association's *Garlic Lover's Cookbook*.

Makes 8 first-course servings

1½ pounds large prawns, peeled
  and deveined (about 16)
⅓ cup clarified butter
4 tablespoons minced garlic
6 green onions, thinly sliced
¼ cup dry white wine
  Juice of 1 lemon (about 2 tablespoons)
8 large sprigs parsley, finely chopped
  Salt and freshly ground pepper to taste
  Lemon slices and parsley sprigs,
    for garnish

Rinse prawns and set aside. Heat clarified butter in large skillet over medium heat. Cook garlic 1 to 2 minutes or until softened but not brown. Add prawns, green onions, wine and lemon juice; cook until prawns turn pink and firm, 1 to 2 minutes on each side. Do not overcook. Just before serving add chopped parsley and season with salt and pepper. Serve on individual shell-shaped or small gratin dishes, garnished with slice of lemon and fresh parsley sprig.

Caviar is a luxury few can afford on a regular basis. Good beluga sturgeon caviar can be outrageously priced and is usually beyond most people's entertaining budget. Now Whitefish caviar, also called golden caviar, is widely available and often priced quite reasonably. The tiny, bright yellow eggs come from Great Lakes Whitefish. This roe is processed similarly to salmon and beluga sturgeon caviar and then flash-frozen for freshness. All types of caviar are best when served very cold and should never be cooked.

Chilled Seafood Lasagna with Herbed Cheese

◆ Marc Waltzer was a prize winner in the Wisconsin Milk Marketing Board Supermarket Chef Showcase.

Makes 24 first-course or 8 entrée servings

    2 cups Wisconsin ricotta cheese
 1½ cups Wisconsin mascarpone cheese*
    2 tablespoons lemon juice
    1 tablespoon minced fresh basil
    1 tablespoon minced fresh dill
    1 tablespoon minced fresh tarragon
  ¼ teaspoon white pepper
    8 lasagna noodles (2 inches wide),
        cooked and drained
    1 pound lox
    4 ounces Whitefish caviar, gently rinsed

Place ricotta cheese, mascarpone cheese, lemon juice, herbs and pepper in food processor container; process until well combined. Line terrine mold with plastic wrap, allowing wrap to come over sides of pan. Layer 1 noodle, ½ cup of the cheese mixture, 2 ounces lox and 2 rounded teaspoons caviar in pan. Repeat layers with remaining ingredients, ending with noodle. Cover; refrigerate several hours or until firm. Carefully remove from mold and remove plastic wrap. Garnish with strips of lox rolled to look like roses and fresh herb sprigs. Slice with warm knife.

Note: Can be prepared without terrine mold. Layer lasagna on plastic wrap. Cover and wrap with foil.

*Mascarpone cheese is a soft, delicate cheese with a buttery-rich flavor and is similar in consistency to whipped cream cheese.

Cheddar Chili Tomato Pots

◆ Marge Walker from Indianapolis, Indiana won first prize in the Appetizer category of the "Sargento® Cheese Makes the Recipe" contest.

Makes 6 first-course servings

 6 medium-size tomatoes
3½ cups (14 ounces) Sargento® Fancy
     Shredded Sharp Cheddar
     Cheese, divided
 2 cans (4 ounces each) chopped mild
     green chilies, well-drained
 ½ teaspoon dried oregano
 ½ teaspoon minced garlic
 6 tablespoons sour cream
 3 green onions, sliced
   Breadsticks, for serving

Preheat oven to 325°F. Grease shallow baking dish. Cut ½-inch slice from top of each tomato; scoop out pulp and seeds, leaving ¼-inch shell (reserve pulp for another use such as salads or sauces). Invert tomatoes on paper towel-lined plate and let drain 20 minutes. Combine 3 cups of the cheese, the chilies, oregano and garlic in medium-size bowl. Divide mixture evenly among tomato shells. Arrange tomato shells in prepared dish; bake 20 minutes. To serve, top with sour cream, remaining ½ cup cheese and the green onions. Serve with breadsticks.

Flounder Ravioli with Mustard-Tomato Sauce

◆ Susan Weisberg from Pleasantville, New Jersey was a prize winner in the "Fabulous Fishing for Compliments" Recipe Contest sponsored by the New Jersey Department of Agriculture, Fish and Seafood Development Program.

Makes 4 first-course servings

½ **pound fresh flounder, cut into chunks**
1 **egg, separated**
⅓ **cup buttermilk**
2 **tablespoons minced parsley**
1 **package (16 ounces) wonton skins**
2 **tablespoons virgin olive oil, divided**
2 **large tomatoes, seeded and chopped**
¼ **cup minced onion**
1 **large garlic clove, minced**
1 **cup** *each* **white wine and water**
1½ **tablespoons** *each* **prepared yellow and spicy brown mustard**
4 **tablespoons butter, cut into pieces**

Process flounder, egg white and buttermilk in food processor or blender until well combined. Stir in parsley; season with salt and pepper. Place heaping teaspoonful of fish mixture in center of wonton skin; moisten edges with beaten egg yolk. Top with another wonton skin and press to seal, working out any air bubbles. Repeat with remaining wonton skins.

Heat 1 tablespoon olive oil in large skillet; add tomatoes and cook briefly. Remove with slotted spoon; set aside. Heat remaining 1 tablespoon oil in skillet; cook onion until tender. Add garlic and cook about 2 minutes. Add wine, scraping up any brown bits. Add water; bring to a boil. Reduce heat; simmer until reduced to ½ cup. Whisk mustards into wine mixture until well blended. Gradually whisk in butter. Reduce heat to low. Season with salt and pepper; add reserved tomatoes. Cook until heated through.

Cook ravioli, a few at a time, in boiling salted water for 5 minutes; drain. Top ravioli with sauce. Garnish as desired.

This surefire method to hard cook eggs comes from the American Egg Board. Place the desired number of eggs in a single layer in a saucepan. Add enough water to come at least 1 inch above the eggs. Cover and quickly bring water just to boiling. Turn off heat. If necessary, remove the pan from the burner to prevent further boiling. Let eggs stand, covered, in the hot water 15 to 17 minutes. Immediately run cold water over eggs or put them in ice water until completely cooled.

Avocado Egg Salad ▶

◆ Daryl Urzen from Pennsylvania won second place in the Adult Division of the National Egg Cooking Contest sponsored by the American Egg Board.

Makes 6 first-course servings

2 tablespoons mayonnaise
2 tablespoons sour cream
1 tablespoon lemon juice
½ teaspoon salt
¼ teaspoon hot pepper sauce
2 avocados, peeled, pitted and chopped
1 cup chopped tomatoes
½ cup chopped red onion
6 hard-cooked eggs, chopped
¼ cup chopped parsley or cilantro

Combine mayonnaise, sour cream, lemon juice, salt and hot pepper sauce in large bowl. Add avocados, tomatoes, onion, eggs and parsley. Toss lightly until well combined. Cover; refrigerate. Serve on spinach leaves.

Zesty Wild Rice Salad ▶

◆ Michele Eklund from Minnesota was a prize winner in the Wild Rice Food Show at the Minnesota State Wild Rice Festival, Kelliher, Minnesota.

Makes about 8 first-course servings

5 cups cooked wild rice
2 cups frozen cooked shrimp, thawed *or* 1 can (9¼ ounces) tuna, drained and flaked
½ cup chopped broccoli
½ cup chopped cauliflower
½ cup cubed cheese
¼ cup diced red bell pepper
¼ cup diced green bell pepper
¼ cup Italian dressing

Combine wild rice, shrimp, broccoli, cauliflower, cheese and peppers in large bowl. Cover; refrigerate. Just before serving, toss gently with dressing. Serve on lettuce leaves.

Mushrooms Mary Louise

◆ Terrance Smith from Newark, Delaware was the first place winner at the Mushroom Cook-Off sponsored by the Pennsylvania Fresh Mushroom Program, Kennett Square, Pennsylvania.

Makes 4 first-course servings

28 medium-size fresh mushroom
 caps, divided
 8 tablespoons butter, melted and divided
 2 ounces scallops, diced
 3 medium-size raw shrimp, peeled, deveined
 and diced
 2 ribs celery, sliced
 ¼ cup finely chopped onion
 6 soft-shell clams, shucked and diced,
 juices reserved
 ⅓ cup white wine
 ⅔ cup bread crumbs
 1 cup hollandaise sauce*

Preheat oven to 350°F. Grease 4 (6-inch) casserole dishes. Slice 4 of the mushroom caps. Melt 1 tablespoon of the butter in large skillet. Add sliced mushrooms; cook and stir until tender. Set aside. Place scallops, shrimp, celery and onion in same skillet with remaining 7 tablespoons butter. Cook over medium heat about 2 minutes or until seafood is fully cooked. Add clams with reserved juices to skillet and simmer 1 minute. Add white wine, then remove from heat. Fold in bread crumbs; set aside. (The mixture will become firm as it stands.)

Place 6 mushroom caps in each prepared casserole dish. Cover mushrooms with stuffing mixture. Bake 10 minutes. Remove from oven and place reserved mushrooms on top of each casserole. Top each with ¼ cup of hollandaise sauce and return to oven just to heat through. Serve hot, garnished as desired.

Use your favorite recipe.

Plentiful "P's" Salad

Since 1970 the people of Athens, Texas have staged the Black-Eyed Pea Jamboree. It's a wildly popular annual celebration that draws crowds of people to join in the fun and games and beat their feet to the sounds of country music. The high point is the judging of the reci-peas, and the winners agree to cook up enough of their concoctions to feed 500 people. Imagine the scene when a winner once produced a Pea-tini, which was (you guessed it) a martini sporting a black-eyed pea on a toothpick!

♦ Anna Ardinger from Dallas, Texas was a second place winner in the salad category of the Black-Eyed Pea Jamboree, Athens, Texas.

Makes 12 first-course servings

4 cups cooked and drained black-eyed peas
2 cups cooked and drained rotini pasta
1 medium-size red bell pepper, chopped
1 medium-size green bell pepper, chopped
1 medium-size purple onion, chopped
2 tablespoons chopped parsley
4 slices Provolone cheese, chopped
4 slices pepperoni or salami, chopped
1 jar (2 ounces) pimiento
1 jar (4½ ounces) whole mushrooms, drained
2 tablespoons dry Italian salad dressing mix
½ teaspoon salt
¼ teaspoon black pepper
½ cup wine vinegar
¼ cup sugar
¼ cup vegetable oil

Combine black-eyed peas, pasta, peppers, purple onion, parsley, Provolone cheese, pepperoni, pimiento and mushrooms in large bowl; set aside.

Combine salad dressing mix, salt and pepper in small bowl. Add vinegar and sugar; mix well. Stir in oil. Add to black-eyed pea mixture; toss lightly until well combined. Cover; refrigerate at least 2 hours before serving. Garnish as desired.

Note: Other vegetables such as cauliflower, broccoli, carrots or celery can be added.

Cream cheese is an American original developed over a century ago. It was first produced commercially by a farmer in upstate New York and used as a spread on breads, crackers and bagels. Few considered using it in any other way and certainly no one gave a thought to cooking with it. Fortunately, this is no longer true.

Southwest Appetizer Cheesecake

♦ Debbie Vanni from Libertyville, Illinois was a prize winner in the Philly "Hall of Fame" Recipe Contest sponsored by Philadelphia Brand® cream cheese.

Makes 10 to 12 first-course servings

⅔ **cup finely crushed tortilla chips**
2 **tablespoons margarine, melted**
1 **cup cottage cheese**
3 **packages (8 ounces each) cream cheese, softened**
4 **eggs**
2½ **cups (10 ounces) shredded sharp natural Cheddar cheese**
1 **can (4 ounces) chopped green chilies, drained**
1 **container (8 ounces) sour cream**
1 **container (8 ounces) jalapeño-Cheddar gourmet dip**
1 **cup chopped tomatoes**
½ **cup chopped green onions**
¼ **cup sliced ripe olives**

Preheat oven to 325°F. Combine tortilla chips and margarine; press onto bottom of 9-inch springform pan. Bake 15 minutes. Meanwhile, place cottage cheese in food processor or blender container; process until smooth. In large bowl of electric mixer, combine cottage cheese and cream cheese, mixing at medium speed until well blended. Add eggs, 1 at a time, mixing well after each addition. Blend in Cheddar cheese and chilies. Pour mixture over baked crust. Return to oven and bake 60 minutes.

Combine sour cream and dip; mix thoroughly. Spread mixture over hot cheesecake; return to oven and continue baking 10 minutes. Remove from oven and let cool slightly. Loosen cake from rim of pan; cool completely before removing rim. Refrigerate cheesecake until ready to serve. Top with tomatoes, green onions and olives before serving.

Jumbo Shells Seafood Fancies

◆ Edith Lehr from Wishek, North Dakota was the second place winner in the Appetizing Appetizers Pasta Contest sponsored by the North Dakota Wheat Commission and the North Dakota Mill, Bismark, North Dakota.

Makes 8 first-course servings

> **1 package (16 ounces) uncooked jumbo-size pasta shells**
> **1 can (7½ ounces) crabmeat, drained, flaked and cartilage removed**
> **1 can (2½ ounces) tiny shrimp, drained**
> **1 cup (4 ounces) shredded Swiss cheese**
> **½ cup salad dressing or mayonnaise**
> **2 tablespoons thinly sliced celery**
> **1 tablespoon finely chopped onion**
> **1 tablespoon finely chopped pimiento**
> **Celery leaves, for garnish**

Add shells gradually to 6 quarts boiling salted water; cook until tender, yet firm. Drain; rinse with cold water, then drain again. Invert on paper towel-lined plate to cool. Combine crabmeat, shrimp, cheese, salad dressing, celery, onion and pimiento in medium-size bowl. If mixture seems too dry, add more salad dressing. Spoon mixture into cooled shells; cover and refrigerate until chilled. Garnish with celery leaves.

A handy tip from the California Tomato Advisory Board: Place an apple in a paper bag along with a tomato to hasten ripening.

Fresh Tomato Pasta Andrew

♦ Dahlia Haas from Los Angeles, California was the first place winner in the California Fresh Market Tomato Advisory Board Contest, Los Angeles, California.

Makes 4 first-course servings

1 pound fresh tomatoes, cut into wedges
1 cup packed fresh basil leaves
2 cloves garlic, chopped
2 tablespoons olive oil
8 ounces Camenzola cheese *or* **6 ounces ripe Brie cheese, cut into small pieces**
2 ounces Stilton cheese, cut into small pieces
Salt and white pepper to taste
4 ounces uncooked angel hair pasta, vermicelli or other thin pasta
Freshly grated Parmesan cheese

Place tomato wedges, basil, garlic and oil in food processor or blender container; process until ingredients are roughly chopped, but not pureed. Combine tomato mixture and cheeses in large bowl; season with salt and pepper. Cook pasta in rapidly boiling salted water until tender, yet firm; drain. Top hot pasta with tomato sauce and serve with Parmesan cheese. Garnish as desired.

FOREIGN FLAIR

Taco Dip

◆ Beth Gostisha was a prize winner in the Wisconsin Milk Marketing Board Supermarket Chef Showcase.

Makes 10 servings

12 ounces cream cheese, softened
½ cup dairy sour cream
2 teaspoons chili powder
1½ teaspoons ground cumin
⅛ teaspoon ground red pepper
½ cup salsa
2 cups shredded lettuce or lettuce leaves
1 cup (4 ounces) shredded Wisconsin Cheddar cheese
1 cup (4 ounces) shredded Wisconsin Monterey Jack cheese
½ cup diced plum tomatoes
⅓ cup sliced green onions
¼ cup sliced ripe olives
¼ cup pimiento-stuffed green olives
Tortilla chips and blue corn chips

Combine cream cheese, sour cream, chili powder, cumin and red pepper in large bowl; mix until well blended. Stir in salsa. Spread onto 10-inch serving platter lined with lettuce. Top with cheeses, tomatoes, green onions and olives. Serve with chips.

The Hindu recipe for Worcestershire sauce was brought to England by Sir Marcus Sandys, a former governor of Bengal. Having eaten the sauce for many years, he was anxious to share it with his friends and have a supply for himself. He took the recipe to a drugstore in Worcestershire, and there the shop owners, Mr. John Lea and Mr. William Perrins, not only recreated the sauce, but soon expanded into larger quarters as the popularity of their condiment spread around the world.

Fried Vegetable Rolls

◆ Tammy Duplessis from Metairie, Louisiana was a finalist in the vegetable division of *The Times-Picayune Cookbook* Recipe Contest.

Makes about 15 appetizers

¼ cup red wine
2 tablespoons teriyaki sauce
2 tablespoons Worcestershire sauce
1 cup *each* diced zucchini and yellow squash
1 cup *each* broccoli and cauliflower flowerets
½ cup diced carrots
¼ cup *each* chopped red onion and parsley
¼ teaspoon white pepper
⅛ teaspoon *each* ground red pepper and
   black pepper
¼ teaspoon garlic salt
1 package (16 ounces) egg roll skins
1 egg, beaten
   Peanut oil, for frying
   Sweet and sour sauce or hot mustard
   sauce, for serving

Combine wine, teriyaki sauce and Worcestershire sauce in large saucepan over medium heat. Stir in vegetables, parsley, peppers and garlic salt. Cook 5 to 10 minutes or until flavors blend; do not overcook. Remove from heat. Allow to cool to room temperature.

Place about 2 tablespoons vegetable mixture on bottom half of egg roll skin. Moisten left and right edges with egg. Fold bottom edge up to just cover filling. Fold left and right edges ½ inch over; roll up jelly-roll fashion. Moisten top edge with egg and seal. Complete all rolls.

Heat about ½ inch of peanut oil in large heavy skillet over medium heat until oil reaches 365°F; adjust heat to maintain temperature. Fry rolls, a few at a time, in hot oil, until golden brown, turning once. Drain on paper towels. Serve warm with sweet and sour sauce or hot mustard sauce for dipping.

Serbian Lamb Sausage Kabobs

♦ Jane Witty Gould from Elizabeth, New Jersey was a prize winner in the "Food Editors' Choice" Recipe Contest sponsored by the American Lamb Council.

Makes 10 servings

1 pound lean ground lamb
1 pound lean ground beef
1 small onion, finely chopped
2 cloves garlic, minced
1 tablespoon hot Hungarian paprika
1 small egg, slightly beaten
   Salt and freshly ground black pepper
      to taste
   Red, green and yellow bell peppers,
      cut into squares
   Rice pilaf (optional)

Combine lamb, beef, onion, garlic, paprika and egg in large bowl; season with salt and pepper. Shape meat mixture into small (about 1-inch) oblong sausages. Place on waxed paper-lined jelly-roll pan and freeze 30 to 45 minutes or until firm; do not freeze completely.

Alternately thread sausages and peppers onto metal skewers. Grill over medium-hot coals 5 to 7 minutes. Turn kabobs taking care not to knock sausages off. Continue grilling 5 to 7 minutes longer or until meat is done. If desired, serve with rice pilaf. Garnish as desired.

Note: The seasonings may be adjusted, but the key to authenticity is the equal parts beef and lamb and the garlic and paprika. You may use sweet paprika if you prefer a milder taste.

Peeling Garlic Cloves

To quickly peel whole garlic cloves, place the desired number of cloves in a small glass custard cup. Microwave at HIGH (100% power) until slightly softened, 5 to 10 seconds for 1 clove or 45 to 55 seconds for a whole head. Then just slip the garlic out of its skin; nothing could be easier! If the cloves are to be minced, trim off the ends and crush with the bottom of a heavy saucepan or the flat side of a large knife. The peels can then be easily removed.

Patrician Escargots

◆ Pat Trinchero from Gilroy, California won third prize in the Great Garlic Recipe Contest sponsored by the Fresh Garlic Association in association with the Gilroy Garlic Festival, Gilroy, California.

Makes 4 servings

- 4 heads garlic,* separated into cloves and peeled
- ½ cup olive oil
- ½ cup butter
- 1 onion, finely chopped
- 1 teaspoon finely chopped fresh rosemary *or* ½ teaspoon dried rosemary
- ¼ teaspoon ground thyme
- 2 dashes ground nutmeg
  Salt and pepper to taste
- 24 large canned snails, drained
- ½ cup chopped parsley
- 24 large fresh mushrooms
- 12 pieces thin-sliced white bread

Finely chop garlic. Heat oil and butter in large skillet over medium heat until butter is melted. Add garlic, onion, rosemary, thyme and nutmeg; season with salt and pepper. Reduce heat to low and add snails and parsley; simmer for 30 minutes, stirring occasionally.

Preheat oven to 350°F. Remove stems from mushrooms. Arrange mushroom caps upside down in 2-inch-deep baking dish; place 1 snail in each mushroom cap. Pour garlic mixture over snails; cover with foil and bake 30 minutes. While snails are baking, remove crusts from bread slices. Toast each slice and cut diagonally into 4 triangles. Serve with escargots.

*The whole garlic bulb is called a head.

Pasta is favored by dieters and athletes alike. It is rich in energizing complex carbohydrates and essential B vitamins. Because complex carbohydrates are digested slowly they help to curb the appetite and sustain body energy. Low in fat and cholesterol, pasta is easy to prepare and goes with almost any meal. With the multitude of shapes, sizes and colors available today, no wonder pasta is showing up on dinner tables everywhere.

Italian Veggie Salad

◆ Pauline M. Anisman from Houma, Louisiana was a finalist in *The Times-Picayune Cookbook* Recipe Contest.

Makes 8 to 10 servings

1 package (8 ounces) fettucini or spaghetti
1 jar (6 ounces) marinated artichoke hearts
1 can (6 ounces) ripe olives, drained
2 small carrots, shredded
1 small zucchini, halved lengthwise
   and sliced
1 small green bell pepper, sliced into
   thin rings
1 package (3 ounces) pepperoni, thinly sliced
1 cup (4 ounces) shredded mozzarella cheese
¼ cup grated Parmesan cheese
1 tablespoon grated Romano cheese
2 tablespoons vegetable oil
2 tablespoons vinegar
½ teaspoon fennel seeds
½ teaspoon Dijon-style mustard
2 cloves garlic, minced
1 medium-size avocado, peeled, pitted
   and sliced
1 medium-size tomato, chopped
   Additional grated Parmesan cheese

Cook fettucini according to package directions; drain and set aside. Drain artichoke hearts, reserving liquid; chop. Combine cooked fettucini, artichokes, olives, carrots, zucchini, green pepper, pepperoni, and cheeses in large bowl; set aside.

Combine reserved artichoke liquid, oil, vinegar, fennel seeds, mustard and garlic in screw-top jar. Shake well. Pour over fettucini mixture. Toss well. Cover; refrigerate until thoroughly chilled.

Just before serving, add sliced avocado and chopped tomato. Sprinkle with additional Parmesan cheese. Garnish as desired.

Picante Black Bean Soup

♦ Katheryn Gonzales from Park Forest, Illinois won first prize in the Soups and Stews category of the Pace® Picante Sauce "Pick Up the Pace" Recipe Contest sponsored by Pace Foods, Inc.

Makes 6 to 8 servings

   4 slices bacon, diced
   1 large onion, chopped
   1 clove garlic, minced
   2 cans (15 ounces each) black beans,
      undrained
   1 can (about 14 ounces) beef broth
1¼ cups water
   ¾ cup Pace® picante sauce
   ½ to 1 teaspoon salt
   ½ teaspoon oregano leaves, crushed
      Sour cream
      Additional Pace® picante sauce and
      crackers

Cook bacon over medium-high heat in large saucepan until crisp. Remove to paper towels; set aside. Add onion and garlic to drippings; cook and stir 3 minutes. Add beans, broth, water, 3/4 cup picante sauce, salt and oregano. Cover and simmer 20 minutes. Ladle into soup bowls; dollop with sour cream. Sprinkle with reserved bacon. Serve with additional picante sauce and crackers.

Arrowroot is a thickening agent coming from a plant native to West India. It has almost no taste and more thickening power than flour or cornstarch. Since it thickens at lower temperatures it can be used in delicate sauces. If arrowroot is unavailable cornstarch can be substituted using 1½ teaspoons of cornstarch for every 1 teaspoon of arrowroot.

Both oriental sesame oil, a strong-tasting oil made from sesame seeds, and rice wine vinegar, a mild, slightly sweet vinegar, can be found in the imported (Oriental) section of the supermarket or in specialty food shops.

Microwave Oriental Relish Dip

◆ Mr. Lynn Whately from Double Springs, Alabama was the fifth place winner in the *Weight Watcher's Magazine* recipe contest sponsored by the Florida Tomato Committee.

Makes 16 servings

  1 **cup peeled chopped tomato**
  ¼ **cup soy sauce**
  ¼ **cup drained canned crushed pineapple**
  1 **tablespoon sugar**
  1 **tablespoon finely chopped red bell pepper**
  1 **tablespoon finely chopped green onion**
  1 **tablespoon minced garlic**
  2 **teaspoons fresh lemon juice**
1½ **teaspoons grated fresh ginger**
  2 **teaspoons rice wine vinegar**
  1 **teaspoon sesame oil**
  1 **teaspoon arrowroot**
  4 **cups plain low-fat yogurt**
  1 **cup creamy peanut butter**
  8 **cups assorted fresh vegetables**

Combine tomato, soy sauce, pineapple, sugar, red pepper, onion, garlic, lemon juice and ginger in 1-quart glass measuring cup. Microwave at HIGH (100% power) 8 minutes; stir every 2 minutes. Stir in rice wine vinegar and sesame oil. Microwave 2 to 3 minutes or until ingredients are reduced to 1 cup. Stir in arrowroot. Cool slightly. Store relish covered in glass container in refrigerator.

To make dip: Combine relish with yogurt and peanut butter in large bowl; mix until well blended. Serve with assorted vegetables.

To make one serving of dip: Combine ¼ cup plain low-fat yogurt, 1 tablespoon peanut butter and 1 tablespoon relish. Serve with ½ cup assorted vegetables.

Notes: Relish is also great mixed with reduced-calorie mayonnaise and used as a sandwich spread or salad dressing.

Microwave ovens vary in wattage and power output; cooking times may need to be adjusted.

SNACK TIME

Popcorn is believed to be the world's oldest form of corn, at least 7,000 years old. The Native Americans brought popcorn to the first Thanksgiving in 1621 and amazed the Pilgrims by heating it up with a little oil and transforming the hard inedible kernels into a delicious fluffy white snack.

Fall Harvest Popcorn

♦ Peggy Meuli from Hope, Kansas was the first place winner in the Appetizers category in the annual recipe contest sponsored by the *Reflector-Chronicle*, Abilene, Kansas.

Makes 2½ quarts

> **2 quarts freshly popped popcorn, unsalted**
> **2 cans (1¾ ounces each) shoestring potatoes (3 cups)**
> **1 cup salted mixed nuts**
> **¼ cup butter or margarine, melted**
> **1 teaspoon dill weed**
> **1 teaspoon Worcestershire sauce**
> **½ teaspoon lemon-pepper seasoning**
> **¼ teaspoon garlic powder**
> **¼ teaspoon onion powder**

Preheat oven to 325°F. Combine popcorn, shoestring potatoes and nuts in large roasting pan. Set aside. Combine butter, dill, Worcestershire sauce, lemon-pepper seasoning, garlic powder and onion powder in small bowl; pour over popcorn mixture, stirring until evenly coated. Bake 8 to 10 minutes, stirring once. Cool completely; store in airtight containers.

Canned chilies should be rinsed in cold water before using. Much of the "fire" is in the seeds and canning liquid. The hotness of chilies is rated on a scale of 1 to 200—with 1 being the mildest. A jalapeño chili, hot enough to burn your mouth, bring tears to your eyes and make your hair curl, rates only 15 on this scale! Taste all chilies very warily if you are a novice.

Southwestern Chili Rellenos

◆ Dan Gerlock was a prize winner in the Wisconsin Milk Marketing Board Supermarket Chef Showcase.

Makes 6 servings

    2 tablespoons olive oil
    ½ teaspoon white pepper
    ½ teaspoon salt
    ½ teaspoon ground red pepper
    ¼ teaspoon ground cloves
    4 cans (4 ounces each) whole green chilies,
        drained, seeded
 1½ cups (6 ounces) shredded Wisconsin
        Cheddar cheese
 1½ cups (6 ounces) Wisconsin Monterey Jack
        cheese
    1 package (16 ounces) egg roll skins
    1 egg yolk
    1 teaspoon water
      Vegetable oil

Combine olive oil and seasonings in small bowl. Add chilies; toss to coat. Let stand 1 hour. Combine cheeses in another small bowl.

For each chili rellenos, place 1 chili in center of 1 egg roll skin; top with ¼ cup cheese mixture. Brush egg roll skin with combined egg yolk and water. Fold two opposite edges over filling, overlapping edges; press together. Press together ends, enclosing filling.

Heat about 3 inches of peanut oil in large heavy saucepan over medium-high heat until oil reaches 375°F; adjust heat to maintain temperature. Fry chili rellenos, a few at a time, in hot oil 2 to 3 minutes or until golden brown. Drain on paper towels.

Onion Flatbread

◆ David A. Sledd from New Orleans, Louisiana was a finalist in the Bread, Rolls and Biscuits category of the *The Times-Picayune Cookbook* Recipe Contest.

Makes 2 flatbreads (6 to 8 servings each)

2⅓ cups warm water (105° to 115°F), divided
 ½ cup plus 3 tablespoons honey, divided
1½ packages dry yeast
 6 tablespoons olive oil, divided
 ⅓ cup cornmeal
 3 cups whole wheat flour
 2 tablespoons coarse salt
 3 to 4 cups all-purpose flour, divided
 2 large red onions, thinly sliced
 1 cup red wine vinegar
 1 cup grated Parmesan cheese
   Freshly ground pepper to taste

Combine ⅓ cup of the water and 3 tablespoons of the honey in large bowl; sprinkle yeast over water. Let stand about 5 minutes until bubbly. Add remaining 2 cups water, 3 tablespoons olive oil, the cornmeal and whole wheat flour. Mix until well blended. Stir in salt and 2 cups of the all-purpose flour. Gradually stir in enough remaining flour until mixture clings to sides of bowl. Turn out onto lightly floured surface. Knead in enough of the remaining flour to make a smooth and satiny dough, about 10 minutes. Halve the dough. Place each half in a large, lightly greased bowl; turn over to grease surface. Cover and let rise in warm place (85°F) until doubled.

Meanwhile, combine onions, vinegar and remaining ½ cup honey. Marinate for at least 1 hour. Grease 2 (12-inch) pizza pans and sprinkle with additional cornmeal. Stretch and pat out dough; with fingertips create valleys. Cover and let dough rise for 1 hour. Dough will double in size. Drain onions and scatter them over dough. Sprinkle with remaining 3 tablespoons olive oil and Parmesan cheese; season with freshly ground pepper. Preheat oven to 400°F. Bake for 25 to 30 minutes until flatbread is crusty and golden. Serve warm.

Oven-Fried California Quesadillas

◆ Sally Vog from Springfield, Oregon was the first place winner in the Appetizers and Snacks category of the Pace® Picante Sauce 40th Anniversary Recipe Contest sponsored by Pace Foods, Inc.

Makes 32 appetizers

2½ cups (10 ounces) shredded Monterey Jack cheese
  1 jar (6 ounces) marinated artichoke hearts, drained and chopped
  1 can (2¼ ounces) sliced ripe olives, drained
  ⅔ cup Pace® picante sauce
  ½ cup chopped toasted almonds
  ¼ cup loosely packed, chopped cilantro
  8 flour tortillas (7- to 8-inch)
  3 tablespoons butter or margarine, melted
    Additional Pace® picante sauce and lime wedges

Preheat oven to 450°F. Combine cheese, artichokes, olives, ⅔ cup picante sauce, the almonds and cilantro in large bowl; mix well. Brush one side of 4 tortillas with butter; place buttered side down on baking sheet. Place 1 cup cheese mixture on each tortilla; spread to within ¾ inch of edge; top each with remaining tortillas, pressing firmly. Brush tops of tortillas with butter.

Bake about 10 minutes or until tops are lightly browned. Remove from oven; let stand 3 to 5 minutes. Cut each quesadilla into 8 wedges. Serve with additional picante sauce and lime wedges.

Salmon Puffs ▶

♦ Michelle Lattman from New York was a prize winner in the Polly-O® International Recipe Competition sponsored by the Pollio Dairy Products Corporation.

Makes 6 servings

  8 ounces Polly-O® ricotta cheese
  1 can (16 ounces) salmon, drained and flaked
  ¼ cup coarsely chopped green bell pepper
  ¼ cup chopped onion
  ½ of 10-ounce package frozen chopped spinach, thawed and drained
  ¼ cup chopped pimiento
  1 package (10 ounces) frozen patty shells, thawed

Preheat oven to 450°F. Combine all ingredients *except* patty shells in large bowl; set aside. Roll each patty shell to an 8-inch circle on floured surface. Place equal amounts of salmon mixture in center of each shell. Fold over; seal edges with water. Place on ungreased baking sheet. *Reduce oven temperature to 400°F.* Bake 25 minutes or until golden brown.

Cajun Fried Oysters ▶

♦ Barbara Poisson from Maryland was a prize winner at the St. Mary's County National Oyster Cook-Off in Leonardtown, Maryland.

Makes 3 dozen appetizers

  ¼ to ½ cup hot pepper sauce
  ½ cup butter or margarine, melted
  36 large oysters, shucked and drained
  2 eggs, slightly beaten
  1 cup cracker meal
    Vegetable oil, for frying

Preheat oven to 400°F. Add hot pepper sauce to butter in small saucepan. Bring to a boil; lower heat and simmer until slightly thickened. Keep warm. Dip oysters in eggs; roll in cracker meal. Fry oysters, a few at a time, in 365°F oil until golden brown; drain. Dip oysters into sauce. Place on ungreased baking sheet. Bake 5 minutes. Serve immediately. Garnish.

Dynasty Duckling Pizza Imperiale

◆ Tillie A. Astorino from North Adams, Massachusetts was the first place winner at the Concord National Duckling Cook-Off sponsored by Concord Farms®.

Makes about 16 servings

4 cups cooked rice
½ cup ground pecans or hazelnuts
1 egg, beaten
2½ cups (20 ounces) shredded Swiss cheese, divided
½ cup grated Parmesan cheese, divided
2 tablespoons olive oil
1 whole Concord Farms® duck breast, halved, boned, skinned and cut into bite-size pieces
1 small sweet onion, cut into thin rings
1 small green pepper, cut into thin rings
1 small red pepper, cut into thin rings
4 ounces fresh mushroom caps, thinly sliced
½ cup pitted ripe olives, sliced
1⅓ cups pizza sauce
1 teaspoon *each* Italian seasoning, fresh chopped mint and fresh chopped basil

Preheat oven to 375°F. Combine rice, pecans, egg, ½ cup of the Swiss cheese and ¼ cup of the Parmesan cheese in large bowl. Grease 12-inch pizza pan. Evenly press rice mixture onto bottom and up side of pan to create ½-inch rim. Bake 10 to 12 minutes; set aside to cool.

Heat olive oil over medium heat in large skillet. Add duck, onion, peppers, mushrooms and olives. Cook and stir 5 to 7 minutes.

Spread pizza sauce over cooled rice crust. Layer 1 cup of the Swiss cheese, the duckling mixture, Italian seasoning, mint and basil on pizza sauce. Top with remaining 1 cup Swiss cheese and ¼ cup Parmesan. Bake 15 to 20 minutes. Let cool slightly. Garnish as desired.

Baked Garlic Bundles

♦ Mark Douglas from Riverside, California was the second place winner in the Great Garlic Recipe Contest sponsored by the Fresh Garlic Association in association with the Gilroy Garlic Festival, Gilroy, California.

Makes 24 to 27 appetizers

½ of 16-ounce package frozen phyllo
    dough, thawed
¾ cup butter, melted
3 large heads fresh garlic,* separated
    into cloves and peeled
½ cup walnuts, finely chopped
1 cup Italian-style bread crumbs

Preheat oven to 350°F. Remove phyllo from package; unroll and place on waxed paper. With a pizza cutter or sharp knife, cut phyllo crosswise into 2-inch wide strips. Cover with another sheet of waxed paper and a damp cloth. (Caution: Phyllo dries out quickly if not covered.) Lay 1 strip at a time on a flat surface and brush immediately with melted butter. Place 1 clove of garlic at 1 end. Sprinkle about 1 teaspoon walnuts along length of strip. Roll up garlic clove in strip, tucking in side edges as you go. Brush with more butter. Roll in bread crumbs. Repeat until all but smallest garlic cloves are used. Place bundles on rack in shallow roasting pan and bake 20 minutes.

*The whole garlic bulb is called a head. See page 48 for helpful tips on peeling garlic.

Cheesy Sun Crisps

♦ Mrs. Orlen Sheldon from Washburn, North Dakota was the second place winner in the Sunflower Council Recipe Contest sponsored by the National Sunflower Association.

Makes 4 to 5 dozen crackers

2 cups (8 ounces) shredded Cheddar cheese
½ cup grated Parmesan cheese
½ cup sunflower oil margarine, softened
3 tablespoons water
1 cup all-purpose flour
¼ teaspoon salt (optional)
1 cup uncooked quick oats
⅔ cup roasted, salted sunflower kernels

Beat cheeses, margarine and water in large bowl until well blended; add flour and salt; mix well. Stir in oats and sunflower kernels; mix until well combined. Shape dough into 12-inch-long roll; wrap securely. Refrigerate about 4 hours (dough may be stored up to 1 week in refrigerator).

Preheat oven to 400°F. Lightly grease cookie sheets. Cut roll into ⅛- to ¼-inch slices; flatten each slice slightly. Place on prepared cookie sheets. Bake 8 to 10 minutes or until edges are light golden brown. Remove immediately; cool on wire rack.

Oregano grows in profusion in the Mediterranean, spilling down the hillsides and filling the air with fragrance. Literally translated it means "joy of the mountain."

Southwestern Snack Squares

♦ Sylvia Schmidt from Glendale, Arizona was the first prize winner in the Appetizer and Party Snacks category of the Quaker® Corn Meal "Contemporary Classics" Recipe Contest.

Makes about 15 squares

1¼ cups all-purpose flour
1 cup thinly sliced green onions
¾ cup Quaker® Enriched Corn Meal
1 tablespoon brown sugar
2 teaspoons baking powder
1 teaspoon dried oregano
½ teaspoon ground cumin
¼ teaspoon salt (optional)
1 cup milk
¼ cup vegetable oil
1 egg
1 cup (4 ounces) shredded Cheddar cheese
1 can (4 ounces) chopped green chilies
¼ cup finely chopped red bell pepper
2 slices crisp-cooked bacon, crumbled

Preheat oven to 400°F. Grease 11 × 7-inch baking dish. Combine flour, green onions, corn meal, brown sugar, baking powder, oregano, cumin and salt in large bowl; mix well. Combine milk, oil and egg in small bowl. Add to corn meal mixture; mix just until moistened. Spread evenly into prepared dish.

Combine cheese, chilies, pepper and bacon in medium-size bowl. Sprinkle evenly over corn meal mixture. Bake 25 to 30 minutes or until wooden toothpick inserted into center comes out clean. Let stand 10 minutes before cutting. Cut into 15 squares.

Note: Also great served as a side dish to fish, chicken or pork. Just cut into 8 squares.

PARTY PLEASERS

Fresh ginger is completely different from dry ginger powder both in appearance and flavor. Resembling a gnarled, tan-colored root, fresh ginger adds its own pungency and aroma to foods and is used extensively in the dishes of the Far East. Store fresh ginger indefinitely by peeling and cutting it into small chunks. Put it in a glass jar and add enough dry sherry to cover. Store, covered, in the refrigerator.

Hot 'n' Honeyed Chicken Wings

◆ Mary Lou Newhouse from South Burlington, Vermont won first prize in the Snacks and Appetizers category of the Pace® Picante Sauce "Pick Up the Pace" Recipe Contest sponsored by Pace Foods, Inc.

Makes about 34 appetizers

  3 pounds chicken wings
  ¾ cup Pace® picante sauce
  ⅔ cup honey
  ⅓ cup soy sauce
  ¼ cup Dijon-style mustard
  3 tablespoons vegetable oil
  2 tablespoons grated fresh ginger
  ½ teaspoon grated orange peel
     Additional Pace® picante sauce

Cut off and discard wing tips; cut each wing in half at joint. Place in 13 × 9-inch baking dish. Combine 3/4 cup picante sauce, honey, soy sauce, mustard, oil, ginger and orange peel in small bowl; mix well. Pour over chicken wings. Cover and refrigerate at least 6 hours or overnight. Preheat oven to 400°F. Place chicken wings and sauce in single layer on foil-lined 15 × 10-inch jelly-roll pan. Bake 40 to 45 minutes or until brown. Serve warm with additional picante sauce. Garnish as desired.

Dissolving Gelatin

Gelatin is a wonderful ingredient, but it is often considered difficult to use. A common cause of mishaps is adding the gelatin to a mixture before it is completely dissolved. Here is one foolproof method for dissolving gelatin successfully:

Sprinkle one package of gelatin over ¼ cup of cold liquid in a small saucepan. Let it stand for 1 minute or so to soften and swell. Place the pan over low heat and stir until the gelatin is completely dissolved, about 3 minutes. Run a finger over the spoon to test for undissolved granules. If it is smooth to the touch, the gelatin is completely dissolved; if it feels grainy, continue heating until it feels smooth.

Shrimp Mold

♦ Terry Sue Roberts from Harrisburg, Arkansas was a prize winner in the Hors d'oeuvres category of the Riceland® Rice Cook-Off at the Arkansas Rice Festival.

Makes 1 mold

3 envelopes unflavored gelatin
¾ cup water
1 can (10¾ ounces) cream of shrimp soup
1 package (8 ounces) cream cheese,
  cut into cubes
2 cans (2½ ounces each) shrimp, drained
1 can (7½ ounces) crabmeat, cartilage
  removed, drained
3 cups cooked Riceland® Rice
1 medium-size onion, chopped
1 red bell pepper, chopped
1 cup mayonnaise
¼ cup lemon juice
2 tablespoons Worcestershire sauce
1 tablespoon garlic powder
1 teaspoon black pepper
  Crisp salad greens
  Crackers, for serving

Sprinkle gelatin over water in small bowl; let stand 1 minute. Heat soup over medium heat in medium-size saucepan; add gelatin mixture and stir to dissolve. Add cream cheese; stir until melted. Remove from heat. Add shrimp, crabmeat, rice, onion, bell pepper, mayonnaise, lemon juice, Worcestershire sauce, garlic powder and black pepper; mix well. Lightly spray 6-cup mold with non-stick cooking spray. Pour into prepared mold and refrigerate until firm. To serve, unmold on greens-lined plate; garnish as desired and serve with favorite crackers.

Today, turkey is no longer restricted to the Thanksgiving table. Because it is at least 50% lower in fat than beef, it is masquerading as everything from bologna to hot dogs to ham. Ground turkey and fresh turkey parts, now available year-round in supermarket meat cases, are finding their way to the dinner table with increasing frequency.

Turkey-Cheese Surprises

♦ Aleen Malcolm from New York City, New York was a prize winner in the Polly-O® International Recipe Competition sponsored by the Pollio Dairy Products Corporation.

Makes 6 servings

> 1 **pound ground turkey**
> ½ **cup stuffing mix**
> ½ **cup finely chopped tart apple**
> ½ **teaspoon poultry seasoning**
> 2 **tablespoons grated Parmesan cheese**
>   **Garlic salt and black pepper to taste**
> 1 **tablespoon butter or margarine**
> ½ **cup finely chopped onion**
> 2 **eggs**
> ¼ **cup Polly-O® ricotta cheese**
> 8 **ounces Polly-O® mozzarella cheese,**
>   **cut into ½-inch cubes**
>   **Dry bread crumbs**
>   **Additional grated Parmesan cheese**
>   **Vegetable oil, for frying**
>   **Cranberry sauce, for serving**

Combine turkey, stuffing mix, apple, poultry seasoning and Parmesan cheese in large bowl; season with garlic salt and pepper. Set aside. Combine butter and onion in skillet over medium-high heat. Cook and stir until tender but not brown. Add onion mixture, eggs and ricotta to turkey mixture; blend well. If mixture is too dry, add a little milk.

For each meatball, shape small amount of turkey mixture around a cube of mozzarella. Roll cheese-filled meatballs in a mixture of bread crumbs and additional Parmesan cheese.

Heat ¼ inch oil in heavy skillet over medium-high heat. Fry meatballs, a few at a time, 4 to 5 minutes or until golden brown on all sides. Drain on paper towels. Serve with cranberry sauce. Garnish as desired.

Deep Fried Stuffed Shells

◆ Clarice Moberg from Redstone, Montana was a winner in the Appetizing Appetizers Pasta Contest sponsored by the North Dakota Wheat Commission and the North Dakota Mill, Bismark, North Dakota.

Makes 8 servings

16 uncooked jumbo-size pasta shells
2 eggs, divided
1 can (6½ ounces) tuna, drained and flaked
      ***or* 1 can (6 ounces) crabmeat, drained, flaked and cartilage removed**
1 cup (4 ounces) shredded Cheddar or Swiss cheese
1 medium-size tomato, peeled, seeded and chopped
2 tablespoons sliced green onion
½ teaspoon dried basil, crushed
⅛ teaspoon black pepper
1 tablespoon water
1 cup dry bread crumbs
      Vegetable oil, for frying
      Tartar sauce, for serving

Add shells gradually to 6 quarts boiling salted water and cook until tender, yet firm. Drain; rinse with cold water, then drain again. Set aside to cool.

Slightly beat 1 egg; combine with tuna, cheese, tomato, green onion, basil and pepper in medium-size bowl. Stuff cooked shells with tuna mixture.

Beat remaining 1 egg with water in small bowl. Dip each stuffed shell in egg mixture and roll in bread crumbs. Heat 2 inches oil in large heavy saucepan over medium-high heat until oil reaches 365°F; adjust heat to maintain temperature. Fry shells, a few at a time, in hot oil 1½ to 2 minutes or until golden brown. Drain on paper towels. Serve with tartar sauce. Garnish as desired.

Capers are the small, pea-size bud of a flower from the caper bush. Found mostly in Central America and the Mediterranean, capers add pungency to sauces, dips and relishes. Usually these green buds are pickled and can be found in the condiment section of the supermarket. They taste very much like gherkin pickles.

Liptauer Cheese Appetizer ▶

◆ Dorothy Walsh from New Jersey was a prize winner in the Polly-O® International Recipe Competition sponsored by the Pollio Dairy Products Corporation.

Makes about 2 cups

1 cup Polly-O® ricotta cheese
2 packages (3 ounces each) cream cheese
1 medium-size onion, finely chopped
1 tablespoon capers, drained
1½ teaspoons caraway seeds
2 anchovy fillets, mashed *or* 2 teaspoons anchovy paste
1 teaspoon *each* dry mustard and paprika
2 tablespoons grated Parmesan cheese
2 tablespoons dry vermouth or gin

Cream ricotta and cream cheese together in large bowl. Add remaining ingredients. Cover and refrigerate at least 1 day or up to 1 week to allow flavors to blend. Serve with crackers or crisp vegetables.

White Bean Dip ▶

◆ Jackie Goudeau from Louisiana won first prize in the Appetizer and Snacks category of the Pace® Picante Sauce Young Cooks Recipe Contest sponsored by Pace Foods, Inc.

Makes 1½ cups

1 clove garlic, minced
1 can (15 ounces) great Northern or pinto beans, well drained
1 tablespoon *each* olive oil and lemon juice
½ to ¾ teaspoon ground cumin
½ cup Pace® picante sauce
2 tablespoons thinly sliced green onion

Process garlic, beans, oil, lemon juice and cumin in food processor or blender until smooth. Transfer to serving bowl; stir in picante sauce and green onion. Serve at room temperature, chilled or heated with pita bread and vegetables.

Scallops à la Schaller

♦ Veronica Schrader from Cranbury, New Jersey was a prize winner in the "Fabulous Fishing for Compliments" Recipe Contest sponsored by the New Jersey Department of Agriculture, Fish and Seafood Development Program.

Makes 4 servings

  1 pound bacon, cut in half crosswise
  2 pounds small sea scallops
  ½ cup olive oil
  ½ cup dry vermouth
  2 tablespoons chopped parsley
  1 teaspoon garlic powder
  1 teaspoon black pepper
  ½ teaspoon onion powder
    Dash of oregano
    Salad greens, for serving

Wrap 1 bacon piece around each scallop; if necessary secure with wooden toothpick. Place wrapped scallops in baking dish. Combine olive oil, vermouth, parsley, garlic powder, pepper, onion powder and oregano in small bowl. Pour over scallops. Cover and refrigerate at least 4 hours.

Remove scallops from marinade. Arrange on broiler pan. Broil, 4 inches from heat, 7 to 10 minutes or until bacon is brown. Turn over and brown other side for about 5 minutes. Remove wooden toothpicks. Arrange on platter lined with greens. Garnish as desired.

Carrots have been around since ancient times, but were not widely used until the Middle Ages. At that time, they were red, purple or black in color. It wasn't until the 16th century that a yellow strain became popular. By the next century, in Holland, it had evolved into the familiar orange vegetable we know today.

Twelve Carat Black-Eyed Pea Relish

♦ Lauralyn Murphy from Dallas, Texas was the third place winner at the Black-Eyed Pea Jamboree, Athens, Texas.

Makes 2 to 3 pints

1 cup vinegar
¼ cup vegetable oil
2 cans (15 ounces each) black-eyed peas, drained
12 small carrots, steamed until crisp-tender, coarsely chopped
1 sweet onion, finely chopped
1 green bell pepper, finely chopped
1 cup sugar
¼ cup Worcestershire sauce
2 teaspoons black pepper
2 teaspoons salt (optional)
2 dashes ground red pepper

Combine vinegar and oil in small saucepan. Bring to a boil. Combine black-eyed peas, carrots, onion, green pepper, sugar, Worcestershire sauce, black pepper, salt and ground red pepper in large bowl. Pour oil mixture over vegetable mixture. Cover and refrigerate at least 24 hours to allow flavors to blend. Store covered in glass containers in refrigerator. Serve cold; garnish as desired.

When buying clams in the shell, be sure shells are tightly closed. If the shell is slightly open, give it a light tap. It should immediately snap shut. If it doesn't then the clam is dead and should be discarded. To make opening clams easier, place them on a baking sheet and heat in 300°F oven until they start to open.

Clams Casino

♦ Barbara Huefler from Brick, New Jersey was a prize winner in the "Fabulous Fishing for Compliments" Recipe Contest sponsored by the New Jersey Department of Agriculture, Fish and Seafood Development Program.

Makes about 15 servings

2 dozen medium-size cherrystone clams, scrubbed
8 slices bacon, cut into ½-inch pieces
1 medium-size onion, chopped
1 green bell pepper, chopped
1 cup butter or margarine, softened
¼ cup lemon juice
⅛ teaspoon ground red pepper
¼ cup Italian-style bread crumbs

Open and chop clams, reserving 3 tablespoons clam juice. Reserve clam shells. Cook bacon in skillet over medium-high heat until crisp. Drain on paper towels; set aside.

Preheat oven to 350°F. Discard all but 1 tablespoon bacon drippings. Cook onion and green pepper in same skillet until tender but not brown. Set aside to cool. Combine butter and lemon juice in small bowl; mix well. Add cooked bacon, onion mixture and red pepper. In another small bowl combine clams, reserved clam juice and bread crumbs.

Fill clam shells ½ full with clam mixture and top with 1 tablespoon butter mixture. Bake 20 minutes or until lightly browned. Garnish as desired.

Note: May be frozen before baking. When ready to serve, place frozen clams on baking sheet and increase baking time.

Sour cream will curdle if it becomes too hot and there are no culinary tricks that will restore it. Always add sour cream at the end of the cooking time and heat it only until it is warm, not hot, and never to a boil.

Sesame-Sour Cream Meatballs

◆ Marella Presler from Gackle High School was a winner in the North Dakota High School Beef Bash sponsored by the North Dakota CattleWomen and the North Dakota Beef Commission in cooperation with the State Board for Vocational Education.

Makes 4 dozen meatballs

1½ **pounds ground beef**
⅔ **cup minced onion**
½ **cup fresh bread crumbs**
1 **egg**
¼ **cup milk**
½ **teaspoon salt**
⅛ **teaspoon black pepper**
⅛ **teaspoon ground ginger**
2 **tablespoons vegetable oil**
2 **tablespoons butter or margarine**
½ **cup beef broth**
Sesame-Sour Cream Sauce (recipe follows)
Toasted sesame seeds

Combine ground beef, onion, bread crumbs, egg, milk, salt, pepper and ginger in large bowl. Shape into 1-inch meatballs. Heat oil and butter over medium heat in skillet. Add meatballs and brown on all sides. Add broth. Cover and simmer 5 to 10 minutes. Prepare Sesame-Sour Cream Sauce. Place hot meatballs in serving bowl; top with sauce. Sprinkle with toasted sesame seeds. Garnish as desired.

Sesame-Sour Cream Sauce: Melt 2 tablespoons butter or margarine in small saucepan. Blend in 2 tablespoons all-purpose flour, ½ teaspoon ginger and ¼ teaspoon salt. Cook until bubbly. Add ½ cup beef broth. Cook until thickened, stirring constantly. Add 1 tablespoon soy sauce and 2 tablespoons toasted sesame seeds. Remove from heat; pour into small bowl. Add ¾ cup sour cream, stirring until smooth.

Chilled Seafood Antipasta

◆ T.J. Planteck from Skillman, New Jersey was a prize winner in the "Fabulous Fishing for Compliments" Recipe Contest sponsored by the New Jersey Department of Agriculture, Fish and Seafood Development Program.

Makes 8 servings

12 ounces scallops, cleaned
 7 tablespoons olive oil, divided
 2 teaspoons lemon juice
 1 pound cod fillets, cut into cubes
 1 tablespoon *each* sugar and dry minced
      onion
 1 teaspoon salt
 ½ teaspoon *each* garlic powder, freshly
      ground black pepper and crushed
      red pepper
 1 cup fresh basil leaves, divided
 1 can (6 ounces) small ripe olives,
      pitted, drained
 1 jar (5¾ ounces) Spanish green olives,
      drained
 1 jar (4½ ounces) whole mushrooms, drained
 1 can (8½ ounces) artichoke hearts, drained
12 ounces white Cheddar cheese, cut into
      1-inch chunks
 1 cup vegetable oil
 ⅔ cup vinegar

Cook and stir scallops and 4 tablespoons of the olive oil in large saucepan over high heat 2 to 4 minutes or just until opaque; remove. Stir in lemon juice; set aside. Repeat with remaining 3 tablespoons oil and the cod; remove.

Combine sugar, onion, salt, garlic powder, black pepper and red pepper in small bowl. Place ½ cup basil in 13 × 9-inch dish; sprinkle with half the sugar mixture. Add seafood; layer with olives, mushrooms, artichokes and cheese. Top with remaining sugar mixture and basil. Combine vegetable oil and vinegar; pour over seafood. Cover; refrigerate overnight. Remove and discard basil leaves if desired. Place seafood mixture onto lettuce-lined platter. Garnish as desired.

Egg Champignons

◆ Dorie Black from Lakeview, Arkansas was the third place winner in the Adult Division of the National Egg Cooking Contest sponsored by the American Egg Board.

Makes 24 appetizers

6 hard-cooked eggs, finely chopped
¼ cup dry bread crumbs
¼ cup (1 ounce) crumbled blue cheese
2 tablespoons thinly sliced green onions
**   with tops**
2 tablespoons dry white wine
2 tablespoons butter, melted
1 tablespoon snipped parsley *or*
**   ½ tablespoon parsley flakes**
½ teaspoon garlic salt
24 large fresh mushroom caps (about
**   1½ inches in diameter)**
Paprika (optional)

Preheat oven to 450°F. Lightly grease baking sheet. Combine eggs, bread crumbs, cheese, green onions, wine, butter, parsley and garlic salt in medium-size bowl. Fill each mushroom cap with 1 rounded tablespoon of mixture. Place mushroom caps on prepared baking sheet.

Bake 8 to 10 minutes. If desired, sprinkle with paprika. Garnish as desired.

To check if an egg has been hard-cooked, spin it like a top. If it spins on its end, it is cooked; if it turns on its side, it is raw.

INDEX